C. EVERETT KOOP

C. EVERETT KOOP
The Health of the Nation

by
Anne Bianchi

New Directions
The Millbrook Press
Brookfield, Connecticut

Produced in association with Agincourt Press.
Interior Design: Tilman Reitzle

Photographs courtesy of: AP/Wide World Photos: 10, 12, 17, 47,
51, 54, 59, 65, 69, 72, 86, 93; The Bettmann Archive: 25, 38, 56,
79, 89; Dartmouth College: 33.

Library of Congress Cataloging-in-Publication Data

Bianchi, Anne.
C. Everett Koop: the health of the nation/by Anne Bianchi.

p.   cm.
"New directions."
Includes bibliographical references and index.

Summary: A biography of President Reagan's Surgeon General, a
previously titular position which Dr. Koop used to inform Americans
about such controversial issues as AIDS, smoking, and abortion.

1. Koop, C. Everett (Charles Everett), 1916- .
2. Health officers—United States—Biography—
Juvenile literature. 3. Pediatric surgeons—United States—
Biography—Juvenile literature.
[1. Koop, C. Everett (Charles Everett), 1916-   .
2. Health officers. 3. Physicians.] I. Title.

ISBN 1-56294-103-8

R154.K45B53   1992
610'.92—dc20
[B]   92-1230   CIP

*To Doug, whose constant support
makes every project possible*

Contents

Introduction

Charles Everett Koop always knew that he was going to be a surgeon. As a young boy growing up in Brooklyn, he dreamed of one day being able to cure the sick and heal the wounded. As a teenager, he even pretended to be a medical student so that he could sneak into hospitals and witness operations.

Once he became a surgeon, Koop pioneered the field of pediatric surgery. For thirty-five years, he worked tirelessly to improve surgical procedures for newborns and infants, saving thousands of lives and ensuring better care for future generations. Dr. Koop's groundbreaking efforts quickly made him famous throughout his profession, but it was his work as an anti-abortion activist that brought him to national prominence and attracted the attention of President-elect Ronald Reagan.

When Reagan nominated Koop for the office of Surgeon General, he and the rest of the American public expected that Dr. Koop would continue to lobby against abortion. But Koop confounded everyone's expectations. Once in office, he courageously put aside his personal beliefs to act in the best medical interests of the American people. Rather than use the office of Surgeon General as a bully pulpit for anti-abortion messages, Koop instead raised public consciousness about health.

In tackling controversial issues such as smoking and AIDS, Dr. Koop displayed a level of character and integrity that is rarely seen among government officials. Refusing to follow his party's line in matters of health and medicine, the Surgeon General repeatedly upset conservatives and surprised liberals by resisting the policies and attitudes of the administration that had appointed him. Throughout his eight years in office, Dr. Koop remained a simple physician who took his responsibilities toward his patient—the American people—seriously and refused to compromise their care for the sake of politics.

Caroline Hodges Persell
Chair, Department of Sociology
New York University

Surgeon General of the United States C. Everett Koop

1

Dr. Koop Goes to Washington

Dr. Charles Everett Koop usually worked fourteen-hour days. But on Tuesday, November 4, 1980, the country's most prominent children's surgeon left the hospital early. He and his wife, Betty, had been invited to their son Norman's house to watch the presidential election results on television, and Dr. Koop did not want to be late.

Koop was far from alone in leaving work early that day. The roads were crowded with people rushing home to their television sets, impatient for news. The 1980 election between the incumbent president—Jimmy Carter—and Ronald Reagan, a former governor of California, promised to be a watershed in presidential politics. Who could imagine a more dramatic choice? As a liberal Democrat, Carter believed that government should take an active role in preserving the economic well-being of its citizens, while staying out of their personal lives. Conservative Republicans such as Reagan, however, believed just the opposite—that government should stay out of the economic marketplace, but should take an active role in upholding certain standards of personal morality.

In the months leading up to the election, President Carter had maintained a solid lead in the polls. But during the closing weeks of the campaign, support for Reagan surged, and the race tightened considerably. According to the latest polls, the election was too close to call. Anxiously, people from Florida to Alaska cast their ballots and awaited the returns. On this particular Tuesday, Dr. Koop knew, the coun-

Ronald Reagan holds a newspaper clipping announcing his victory.

try would choose between two well-defined and mutually exclusive futures. But few people besides Koop knew that the doctor's future would also be decided that day. Dr. Charles Everett Koop of the Children's Hospital of Philadelphia was about to step into history.

At Norman's house, the Koop family settled in for what they were sure would be a long night's vigil. Then, sooner than anyone expected, the network anchorman began announcing state-by-state results based on exit polls taken as voters left their polling places: "Texas—Republican, California—Republican, Florida—Republican . . ." The Koops were thrilled as state after state went Republican. By early evening, it was already apparent that Ronald Reagan had won the presidency by one of the largest margins in American history.

Being a conservative Republican himself, Koop naturally favored Reagan. And like many other Americans who voted for the former governor, Koop saw Reagan's election as the beginning of a new era in American history. "As we watched the Reagan landslide," Koop recalled, "I felt an optimism unlike anything I had previously felt on an election evening."[1] But the doctor also had a personal stake in the Republican victory. He knew that Reagan's aides had been considering him for the position of Surgeon General. And now that the Reagan administration had itself become a reality, so too might the job offer.

Reagan's overwhelming victory represented an enormous shift in the American political landscape. Not since 1932 had there been so dramatic a reversal in public policy. In that Depression year, Democratic candidate Franklin D. Roosevelt won the election by building a coalition of politically progressive and economically disadvantaged voters. Women, minorities, and labor unions all played key roles in Roosevelt's victory. Out of that coalition came the New Deal, a liberal consensus on social policy that led directly to such programs as Social Security and unemployment insurance, while leaving most personal issues such as homosexuality and religious practice up to the individual citizen. For nearly fifty years, the country followed the course charted by Roosevelt. Then suddenly it voted for a man who repudiated those policies. Why?

Part of the answer is to be found in the state of the American economy during the late 1970s. For much of his time in office, Jimmy Carter presided over a painful recession. Millions of Americans found themselves out of work, and many more felt their lives to be spinning out of control. Prices were soaring, earnings were down, and people began to believe that America's best days were over. Many voters blamed Carter for their problems and became convinced that he was too weak to get the country's economy back on track. This belief in Carter's weakness was deepened in 1979 when Iranian terrorists stormed the U.S. Embassy in Teheran and took 111 Americans hostage. President Carter vigorously pursued a number of options to win their release, from negotiating with their captors to launching a secret assault, but on Election Day—more than a year after the crisis began—the hostages were still being held captive in Iran.

In this climate of discouragement, Ronald Reagan's promise of a brighter future stirred the imagination of the American public. His campaign commercials declared over and over again that there was nothing wrong with America that strong, new leadership couldn't fix. Whereas Reagan pointedly attacked the legacy of the New Deal, Carter claimed that such social programs as Head Start for underprivileged children and the Job Corps training program had indeed been successful. But Reagan countered with charges of widespread welfare fraud and corruption in government social programs. The old solutions weren't working, Reagan insisted; it was time for a change. The country listened.

Reagan also berated Carter's liberal administration for taking social progressivism too far. According to the conservative view, the social radicalism of the 1960s had nearly destroyed the traditional morality upon which the nation's greatness was founded—and the liberals weren't doing anything to bring that morality back. Conservatives claimed, for instance, that abortion and homosexuality were immoral and ought to be prohibited by law, while school prayer was desirable and ought to be allowed, despite the separation of church and state required by the Constitution.

In his speeches, Reagan called for a return to a simpler time of life—a time when Mom stayed home to take care of the kids while Dad went off to work, a time before divorce when families attended church together, a time of neighbors and neighborhoods before people began locking themselves up in high-security apartment buildings. Reagan himself did not attend church regularly, had divorced his first wife, and had strained relationships with his children, but the country nevertheless seized on his words. While Carter spoke of the need for austerity, Reagan promised a speedy return to the nation's former glory. Americans responded to his message.

Reagan's landslide victory gave him the political mandate he needed. But in order to put his policies into effect, Reagan also needed a government filled with people who shared his conservative agenda. As the head of the executive branch of government, the President has the power to make political appointments throughout his administration. Under President Carter, these positions had been filled by Democrats, most of whom were liberals. President-elect Reagan, of course, planned to replace the Democrats with Republicans.

But finding capable candidates to fill thousands of jobs was no easy task. It took time, much more than the two months between Election Day and the inauguration. So even before the election, Reagan and his running mate, George Bush, hired a staff of recruiters to begin the process. During the summer, these recruiters interviewed candidates for the cabinet, the Office of Management and Budget, the National Security Council, and so on.

Finally, one of them got around to the office of Surgeon General, a relatively unimportant position. The recruitment team, busy with more prominent appointments, could not afford to devote much time or attention to a post three levels below cabinet rank. The team simply needed to find someone with suitable medical credentials whose views were compatible with those of the conservative president.

Someone suggested Dr. C. Everett Koop. A renowned pediatric surgeon, Koop certainly had the medical credentials. More importantly, though, he was a popular and powerful spokesman for the anti-abortion movement, a key element of the conservative constituency.

Koop seemed made to order for the Reagan administration. As a deeply religious Christian, he not only shared the president's "family values," but practiced them as well. In speeches, books, and even films, he denounced abortion as murder and condemned both homosexuals and feminists for the role he claimed they played in the disintegration of the American family. Once he had even called for outlawing "private activity. . .repugnant to the moral sensitivity of the American people."[2] It took just a cursory background check for the recruiters to decide that they had found their man.

One afternoon in August, the phone rang in Koop's office. The doctor took the call. The man on the other end identified himself as John Condon. "I am a headhunter for Reagan-Bush," Condon said. "How would you like to be the Surgeon General?"

"What makes you so sure they'll be elected?" Koop asked Condon. After all, Carter still led in the polls. "Don't worry about that!" Condon replied.[3] Reagan's man sounded confident, but Koop remained unconvinced—until the night of the election, that is.

Candidate Reagan on the campaign trail.

Then, on February 14, 1981, The Secretary for Health and Human Services, Richard Schweiker, called with the official word: The President planned to nominate him to the post of Surgeon General. Until he was confirmed, however, he would serve as the deputy assistant secretary for health. By this time, Koop had become very enthusiastic about joining the Reagan White House, and he immediately accepted the offer. He and Betty quickly settled their affairs in Philadelphia and set off for Washington. The Koops stayed at a Quality Inn for a week while they looked for a place to live. Finally they found a one-bedroom sublet.

Before Dr. Koop could start his new job, however, he needed to be confirmed by the Senate. But Reagan's transition team assured him that confirmation was a mere formality and no cause for concern. The Republicans held the majority in the new Senate, and they would certainly support the president's nominee. Koop had resisted Condon's assurances a few months before, but this time he listened when Reagan's aides told him not to worry.

The job for which Koop had been nominated was, technically, quite limited in scope. As the nation's chief doctor, the Surgeon General had no real authority, not much staff, and almost no formal responsibility. His chief duties included compiling reports on public health issues and advising the White House on health policy. A Washington insider once described the job as "sort of like the Queen of England—a complete figurehead."[4]

Furthermore, the office of Surgeon General had been badly neglected by recent administrations. President Richard Nixon had not even bothered to appoint a Surgeon General, and President Carter had combined the post with that of the assistant secretary for health. As a result, by 1980, the position of Surgeon General had all but disappeared from the political landscape.

That's why official Washington was so shocked when the announcement of Koop's nomination ignited one of the fiercest political fire storms ever to rage in the history of the nation's capital. For the next nine months, during which time Koop's fitness for the office was debated, editorial pages referred to the nominee as everything from "Dr. Kook" to "the most narrowly opinionated man ever nominated for the post." The *San Francisco Chronicle* went so far as to call Koop "a right-wing nut," while the *Boston Globe* labeled him "a religious crackpot." Even *The New York Times*, noted for its restrained language, ran an article on Koop entitled "Dr. Unqualified."

Why was there so much controversy over such an insignificant appointment? In the months after his election, President Reagan named thousands of people to government posts. Why the intense focus on, of all people, Koop? The answer has more to do with the abortion controversy than with Koop himself.

In his confirmation testimony, Koop repeatedly assured the senators on the Labor and Human Resources Committee that, if confirmed, he would not attempt to impose his personal political views on others. But neither the pro-choice liberals nor the anti-abortion conservatives believed him. The pro-choice and anti-abortion forces alike remained convinced that Koop would continue to speak out against abortion and promote his conservative values, just as he had as a private citizen. Time and again, Koop vowed that he would not "continue to be a speaker on the pro-life circuit" nor "use any post that I might have in the government as a pulpit for an ideology."[5] But nobody believed him.

What those involved in the political infighting failed to appreciate, however, was that Dr. Koop had a particularly strong sense of what it meant to be a public servant. Koop believed that government officials, the Surgeon General included, have an obligation to serve the entire nation, not merely those people who share the moral beliefs of the party in power. It did not matter what Koop's personal attitude towards homosexuals was, for instance, if AIDS threatened their health. As Surgeon General, he would be responsible for all Americans, regardless of their lifestyles and personal morality. His job, as he saw it, was to care for people, rather than preach to them. Koop called his philosophy "placing integrity above ideology."[6]

By focusing solely on Koop's abortion-related activities, the Reagan administration—and Koop's opposition as well—severely misjudged the man. Granted, Koop had spent many long hours on the anti-abortion lecture circuit, but he had spent an even longer time—thirty-five years—working tirelessly to promote better public health. At great personal sacrifice, he had devoted his life to improving the medical care available to critically ill children. But few people cared to notice that Koop himself embodied the old, simple values that President Reagan so far had only talked about. If people had been more open-minded, Koop's actions as Surgeon General might not have come as such a surprise. As it turned out, Koop shocked the nation.

In November of 1981, after nearly a year of publicity and bitterness, Dr. C. Everett Koop was finally confirmed as Surgeon General of the United States. For President Reagan, Koop's confirmation was a long-awaited blessing and a problem now best forgotten. He assumed that having placated the anti-abortion movement with the appointment of Koop, the doctor would now fade silently into the background, joining the long line of anonymous Surgeons General before him.

But Dr. Koop did not vanish into obscurity. Instead—against all expectations, except perhaps his own—Charles Everett Koop emerged as one of the most influential and admired members of the Reagan administration. In his eight years in office, Koop radically transformed the way Americans thought about smoking, AIDS, and health care in general. Just as importantly, he stood out as a model of integrity and courage in public office, much to the displeasure of his superiors in the White House. Though a staunch Republican and an even more committed Christian, Koop was able nevertheless to do just what he had promised: to put aside his personal beliefs and act on behalf of all the people, regardless of whether their views conformed to his own.

Dr. Koop simply took his obligations as a doctor and a public servant far more seriously than anyone had imagined he would. It was as a young boy growing up in Brooklyn that Charles Everett Koop first decided to devote his life to health care. That did not change when he became Surgeon General.

2

A Child's Paradise

On October 14, 1916, after ninety-two grueling hours of labor, Helen Apel Koop gave birth to a son in the living room of her Brooklyn home. Miraculously, both mother and child survived. Five years earlier, Helen had given birth to a stillborn child and nearly died herself in the process. Following that experience, her physician advised her to avoid another pregnancy. But Helen and her husband, John Everett Koop, desperately wanted a child and ignored the doctor's warning.

They named their son Charles, after an uncle, and Everett, after his father. At school, the boy was known as Everett, but at home he was neither Charles nor Everett. His father called him "Jim," while the rest of the family referred to him either as "the kid" or "the boy." There was little confusion, however, because he remained the only child in his immediate family.

The young Koop spent his childhood surrounded by family. He lived in a three-generation household with his parents and grandparents, whom he called Grandma and Grandpa Koop. Home was a three-story brick house on Fourteenth Street in South Brooklyn. It was a quiet, shady street that smelled of wisteria. From his bedroom window, Koop could see across to Fifteenth Street and the house of Grandma and Grandpa Apel. Aunts, uncles, and cousins also lived nearby, and during the Thanksgiving and Christmas holidays, the entire family would gather together. Being an only child, Koop relished the times he spent with his cousins and the feeling of being part of a large family.

Family was very important to Koop during his early life, and it profoundly shaped his character. With no siblings to distract him, he developed a close relationship with his parents. His father had never finished high school, but John Everett Koop's lack of formal education never held him back. Instead, he rose to become an assistant vice-president of one of the country's largest banks. Always eager to educate his son, the elder Koop would often skip lunch in order to visit the New York Public Library and research questions his son had asked.

John Koop was a kind man, but he also had great strength of character. Once when his son was home from college, John Koop heard the boy talking to his mother about his father's smoking habits. John smoked nearly three packs of cigarettes a day, and his wife feared that the cigarettes were killing him. This was long before the hazards of smoking were widely known, but Helen knew from her husband's hacking cough that the cigarettes must be damaging his health.

She wanted to find a way to make him quit, but her son told her to forget it. He didn't believe his father had the will to stop. When John Koop overheard this remark, he marched upstairs without saying a word and threw his cigarettes down the toilet. He never smoked one again.

Helen Koop also had great impact on her son's development, showering her only child with love and attention. She told him he could accomplish anything and pushed him to strive for excellence. Helen herself was intelligent and well-read, working as a secretary and business manager at a time when most women were excluded from professional life. But Koop always thought that his mother should have been a nurse or a doctor. She was extremely warm and compassionate, and she even had some medical experience, having administered anesthesia during surgeries performed in neighbors' homes. In-home surgeries were fairly common early in this century, and the anesthesia was administered by whoever was willing. Koop would later remember his mother's descriptions of these risky procedures.

Koop's two grandfathers were also critical in his decision to become a surgeon. Grandpa Apel had come to the United States from Germany at the age of 10. When he was old enough, he became an apprentice to a tinsmith and later developed his own roofing and ventilation business. He particularly enjoyed driving his grandson around the neighborhood so that he could point out all the roofs he had built. Grandpa Koop was also a craftsman, a fine engraver of silver and gold. He made his living as a mailman, but engraving was his passion, especially pocket watches. He was always doodling, drawing watch-sized circles and then decorating them with intricate patterns.

"I have often thought that having two grandfathers who were so facile with their hands shaped my desire to use my own hands as a surgeon," Koop has said. "Perhaps I treasured the satisfaction such activities seemed to give them; perhaps it lay in the genes."[1]

For Koop, Brooklyn was a child's paradise. He spent his days at Public School 124 and his afternoons exploring. A scooter gave him his first taste of adventure at the age of 7, after which he graduated to roller skates, which he bought himself for $1.65. One day, soon after making his purchase, Koop skated alongside his father as John Koop walked to an appointment at his dentist's office four miles away. While his father sat in the dentist's chair, Koop skated around nearby Prospect Park and then headed home again. Swelling with pride, he announced to his grandfather that he had worn out two wheels in only one day.

Koop also played sports whenever he could, including stickball on Fourteenth Street and sandlot baseball in Prospect Park with his team, the Conquerors. On weekends, he went on fishing expeditions to a pond in a local cemetery or to the East River docks. On cold winter days, his parents knew they could usually find him in Prospect Park ice skating on the frozen lake.

The crowning jewel of the Brooklyn wonderland, however, was Coney Island, where the smell of grilling hot dogs and the shouts of happy people wafted through the clean ocean air. Swarms of strollers crowded the beaches, the boardwalks, and the amusement parks, the most magnificent in the world, where visitors could experience every kind of thrill imaginable.

The Coney Island boardwalk in the 1920s.

Koop found himself particularly attracted to the "freak shows," which were well known for their outrageous sense of spectacle. There were sword swallowers, the Snake Woman, the Tattooed Man, the Fat Lady, and even a two-headed calf. But Koop was most interested in an exhibit of premature babies being kept alive in incubators. He sat for hours staring at those tiny babies in their heated plastic bubbles.

Yet Koop's childhood was not entirely idyllic. A shy, quiet boy, he did not have many friends and spent most of his time alone or with his family. He was an excellent student; he even skipped a year of junior high school. But Koop always felt like an outsider. "I was the oddball, no matter how you looked at it," he recently admitted.[2]

Walking home from school, Koop was beaten up nearly every day by older boys loitering on street corners. He began changing his lunch money into nickels so that he could duck into phone booths and make calls until the boys outside got tired of waiting for him and went away. It was not until high school that Koop finally emerged from his shell. His high school, the Flatbush School, was a much more welcoming environment than his previous schools had been. Because the school was very small, it was easy for Koop to get to know his classmates. Koop's teachers also encouraged him to involve himself in school activities, so he joined the baseball, basketball, and wrestling teams. His real love, however, was football, and in his senior year he led his team to an undefeated season. On the academic side, Koop joined the debating team and became editor of the school newspaper. In his senior year, he was even elected student body president.

The Flatbush School gave him the confidence he needed to pursue what had by now become his overriding career goal. In his senior essay, Koop wrote, "Now at sixteen I picture myself a great surgeon being consulted by other surgeons no less great. Nothing, it seems, would give me a bigger thrill and would please me more."[3]

From a remarkably young age, Koop had known he wanted to be a doctor. In fact, by the time he was 6 years old, his mind was made up. As a young boy, Koop had been fascinated by the large black bag that Dr. Wright, the family doctor, always brought with him when he came to make a house call. Another doctor who made a great impression on him was Dr. Strong, the family orthopedist. He could set broken bones so gently and carefully, Koop said, that it didn't even hurt. To Koop, Dr. Strong was a role model. "I wanted his gentleness when I became a doctor," Koop once wrote.[4]

Both these men stimulated his interest in medicine, but the desire to become a surgeon was his own. According to Koop, "The idea of using my mind, then my hands, to heal someone simply fascinated me."[5] Even as a young child, he began training his hands to perform the difficult tasks required of a surgeon. He would cut out intricate designs from magazines, using one hand and then the other to follow the sharp curves and angles. He also practiced tying one-handed knots in sewing thread. But he still longed to see a real operation. At the age of 12, Koop convinced one of his father's customers, who was a practicing surgeon, to allow him to observe an operation. The surgeon took Koop right into the operating room with him while he reset a patient's broken nose.

Two years later, at the age of 14, Koop began making subway trips on Saturday mornings to Columbia Presbyterian Hospital in Manhattan, where he would regularly view operations by posing as a medical student. His neighbor, Paul Strong—then a medical student at Columbia—told Koop how to enter the hospital secretly through a side door.

Once in the hospital, Koop would ride the elevator up to the laboratory where Paul worked, from which he would emerge a few seconds later dressed in a white lab coat. Dressed as a medical student, he would sit for hours in the surgical gallery, watching doctors perform operation after operation.

After familiarizing himself with the basic surgical techniques, Koop began to try them himself at home. In his own makeshift operating theater in the basement of his house, Koop kept a supply of rabbits, rats, and stray cats. With his mother's help, he would anesthetize these animals and then operate on them. Koop insisted that he never lost a single patient.

It wasn't until the age of 16, however, that Koop got his first job in medicine. He and his family were spending the summer in Port Jefferson on Long Island when Koop heard about a job in the laboratory of the local hospital. Koop jumped at the opportunity and spent the rest of the summer working at Mather Memorial. Koop enjoyed himself so much that he returned to Mather each summer until his graduation from college four years later.

3

The Making of a Doctor

Charles Everett Koop peered out of the car window at the rolling hills of New Hampshire with wide-eyed expectation. It was a cloudy September morning in 1933, but not even the weather could dampen his enthusiasm. The 16-year-old was leaving home to embark on a new adventure. His destination: Dartmouth College.

Entering the campus, he was awed by the majestic brick buildings and manicured green lawns. He could not imagine any greater thrill than to be where he stood at that moment. All summer, he had been preparing himself, memorizing the school songs and planning his course schedule for what would be the first step on his path to a brilliant surgical career.

With his fine academic record, Koop could have taken his pick of the Ivy League schools, but he chose Dartmouth because of its medical school. He had considered Princeton, which was much nearer his home, but Princeton did not have a medical school. Leaving his tight-knit family was not a welcome prospect, but his future as a surgeon was his first priority. So he was off to Dartmouth, located five hours north in Hanover, New Hampshire.

His years at Dartmouth changed Koop's life forever. And the first thing to go was his name. "Jim," "kid," and "boy" were immediately out, and he never did like the name Everett, so he had no objections when his classmates at Dartmouth nicknamed him "Chick." It was a name that would stick with him for the rest of his life.

Also at Dartmouth, Chick Koop got his first taste of fame, and it came on the football field. In the first few days of team practice, the coach of the Big Green couldn't help noticing Koop's natural ability. Even though he was only a freshman, Koop became the team's starting center and instantly became a school hero. Suddenly, everyone on campus knew his name and looked at him with a mixture of envy and admiration. Upperclassmen invited him to sit with them during meals in the cafeteria, and even faculty members took notice of him.

But Chick's celebrity was short-lived. Only a few weeks after joining the team, he suffered a sharp blow to the head during a practice scrimmage. Chick was knocked unconscious for several minutes and when he finally came to, he realized that something had happened to his vision. When he looked around, he was seeing two of everything. At first, he assumed it to be only a temporary condition. But when, a few days later, the condition had still failed to improve, he went to see a doctor.

After examining Koop, the school ophthalmologist told him that his double vision was permanent but could be corrected with special eyeglasses, which he would have to wear for the rest of his life. Then the doctor asked his patient what he was studying at Dartmouth. "I'm premed," Koop responded. "You're premed and you play this foolish game of football?" the doctor asked. "Let me see your hands." Chick held out his hands, palms up, so the doctor could examine them. "They're beautiful. They're surgeon's hands. So you not only risk your sight and maybe your life, but your hands and your career. Such foolishness."[1]

That was it. Nothing was important enough to endanger his career. Much as he hated to give up his status as a football star, he would not risk his future as a surgeon. The next day, Koop marched into the coach's office and announced that he was quitting the team. The coach tried to change his mind, but Chick refused to reconsider his decision.

With football out of the way now, there was nothing to distract Chick from his studies. He majored in zoology and became a research assistant with the department. The research job allowed him to learn more about his major while making some money to replace the football scholarship he had lost when he quit the team.

Between his schoolwork and his job, Chick had little time for anything else. But what free time he did have, he spent enjoying the mountains of New Hampshire. The first time he put on skis as a freshman, he fell in love with the sport. Every spare moment he spent on the slopes. But once again, his passion for sport almost cost him his career.

During a ski jump competition his sophomore year, Chick took a bad fall that left him temporarily paralyzed. In the middle of a somersault, he landed flat on his back, unable to move. As he lay in bed in the infirmary, he still could barely move his arms and legs. Overcome by panic, he was sure he had lost his surgical career forever.

As it turned out, Koop had suffered nothing more serious than a minor spinal concussion, and his nervous system returned to normal within a few days. But none of his doctors or nurses bothered to explain the condition to him at the time; they let their patient assume the worst. It was an experience that Koop would never forget. He vowed that he would never allow his own patients to suffer the uncertainty and fear that he had.

The most memorable event of Chick's junior year, however, was much more pleasant. It was the weekend of the Winter Ball when he met his future wife, Betty Flanagan. His fraternity brother, Dan Barker, had invited Betty up from Vassar College for the dance. Dan had met her the previous summer, and they had kept in touch.

Chick fell in love with Betty the moment he ran into her in the hallway of his fraternity house. Dan was upstairs napping, so Chick offered to show Betty around the campus. They spent the rest of the afternoon together, talking about their futures, marriage, children. By the end of the day, Chick knew that Betty was the woman he wanted to marry.

A week later, he sent Betty an unsigned valentine. But though he thought of her often, he didn't speak to her again until the spring. Returning to Hanover from a brief trip to New York City in May, Chick decided to make a detour to Vassar College to find Betty. Two days later, Chick called his mother to announce that he was engaged.

Chick Koop entered his senior year confident and optimistic about his future. He had found the woman of his dreams and done so well in his premed studies at Dartmouth that he would certainly be accepted at a medical school for the fall. His first choice was Columbia University's College of Physicians and Surgeons. He had always known Columbia was the place for him. He had posed as a medical student there, and now, eight years later, he really would be one.

Koop arrived for his admissions interview at Columbia full of hope and promise, but it did not go as he had planned. The interviewer asked him whether he expected to make any major medical discoveries. Chick said that he hoped to, but if not, he would be glad to lay the groundwork for others. "We don't think you've got the stuff we are looking for at the College of Physicians and Surgeons!" the interviewer proclaimed.[2] And that was that.

CHARLES EVERETT KOOP
489 Rugby Rd., Brooklyn, N. Y.
FLATBUSH HIGH SCHOOL
Zoology
ΑΣΦ. Zeta Alpha Phi, President.

Chick Koop as he appeared in the 1937 Dartmouth College yearbook.

With one sentence, Koop's vision of the future was shattered. He had never seriously considered another medical school, but just as a precaution, he had scheduled an interview with the Cornell University Medical College, also in New York City. Discouraged by his experience at Columbia, he arrived at Cornell expecting similar treatment. But as soon as he walked through the doors, he felt a difference in attitude. The people at Cornell seemed warm and encouraging, so much so that by the end of the day he had been offered a place in the next year's class. Chick accepted immediately. He knew he would feel at home there.

Chick's instincts about Cornell were right. He loved the school, the people, the classes. But he missed Betty terribly. During his first year of medical school, they visited each other as often as possible, but Vassar, in Poughkeepsie, New York, was some distance away. Still, they persevered and by the following summer, the couple was making wedding plans. Having little money to spend on the wedding, they decided to make it a simple, informal affair. Chick and Betty were married on September 19, 1938, at Vassar in front of their parents, their grandparents, Betty's brother George, and two close friends.

At that time, most medical schools strongly advised married students not to enroll, and some even forbade it. It was assumed that marriage would distract the students from their studies. But Chick and Betty managed nevertheless, because from the beginning they were both completely committed to Chick's medical career. As the daughter of a doctor, Betty knew the sacrifices they would have to make, as well as the future that lay ahead for her as a doctor's wife.

First, there was Chick's grueling work schedule. He spent at least fourteen hours a day, six days a week at the hospital, and then he continued his studies at home. On Sunday, his only day off, he would awaken with severe migraine headaches. Because he suffered these headaches only on Sundays, Chick concluded that relaxation made him sick. He decided that the only possible cure was to convince his body that he was still working. "Tell me I've got a lot to do," Chick would tell Betty as the weekend drew near. "Say it loud so my body will hear."[3] Later, he just stopped taking days off.

The Koops also had to be very careful with money. Their only income was the small salary Betty earned as a secretary at the hospital attached to Cornell's medical school. The Koops even walked back and forth from work each day to save money on transportation. They lived in a small, dark, forty-eight-dollar-a-month apartment and scraped by on only five dollars a week for food.

There was no time and no money for recreation or vacations. During the summers, Chick took internships in other hospitals, while Betty continued to work as a secretary. The summer after their marriage, they lived in Port Jefferson, where Chick had two non-paying hospital jobs. To support them, Betty traveled six hours each day on the Long Island Railroad to and from her job in the city.

But despite the hardships of those early years, the Koops lived very happily. Chick adored medical school from the start, and even more so once he was married. The young medical student was particularly thrilled by a two-week rotation he had in obstetrics during his fourth year. He practically lived at the Berwind Free Maternity Clinic in Harlem, delivering babies. It was intensive training. He delivered a baby a day for fourteen days. Since few of the mothers had received prenatal care, many of their babies were born with complications. But few were ever treated. Chick was surprised to find out that so little was known about the cause and treatment of birth defects.

In June, 1941, Chick graduated from the Cornell University Medical College. After four difficult years, he was finally Dr. Koop. And now that he had finished his medical training, Koop planned to return to his roots in Brooklyn to practice. Two of the best internship programs in the country were located there, at Brooklyn Hospital and Methodist Episcopal Hospital. Both programs, however, had a strong bias against married interns, and both rejected him. A third school, Vanderbilt University in Nashville, Tennessee, even sent him a letter saying, "Dear Koop, you didn't say whether or not you are married. If you are, don't answer this letter."[4]

These rejections, however, turned out to be blessings in disguise, because they led Koop to Philadelphia. He applied to the program at Pennsylvania Hospital, and this time he removed his wedding ring before the interview. But Dr. Ravdin of Pennsylvania Hospital was not concerned with Dr. Koop's marital status. All he wanted to know was whether Koop could handle the rigors of the internship program. Chick told him that if other people had done it, so could he. Ravdin took Koop's word for it and told him to report to Pennsylvania Hospital on July 1. The year was 1941.

4

A New Home

Chick Koop was glad to have found a good internship, but he was less than happy about moving to Philadelphia. First, it would mean being separated from Betty for the first time since their wedding. There were still three months left on their New York lease, and the couple could not afford two rents. So Betty would have to live and work in New York until October, while Chick lived at the hospital. Koop was also depressed about leaving New York for a strange city and by the many years of training that lay ahead of him.

Although he was now a doctor, he still had a long way to go before becoming a surgeon. There was first a two-year internship, then two years operating in a lab, then five more years in surgical training. All told, he was nine years away from becoming a full-fledged surgeon. It seemed an eternity.

The weather his first day in Philadelphia did nothing to improve his mood. He sweated under the sticky, summer sun as he lugged his bags to his new quarters. When he opened the door to his home for the next three months, he saw a single room, cramped and sterile. Koop later wrote that at this moment he felt a strong impulse to repack his bags and jump on the first train back to New York. But he resisted the thought. And as soon as he reported for duty, his attitude changed.

Each day he spent as an intern at Pennsylvania Hospital, and later as a resident at the University of Pennsylvania, the more fortunate he felt to be there. In almost no time, Koop became convinced that these were two of the country's finest hospitals, and he was proud to be associated with them.

And it didn't take Koop very long to feel at home in Philadelphia. Once Betty rejoined him, the couple moved to a charming suburb called Penn Valley, where they made their home. Over the next forty years, Koop grew very attached to the place. Even several years after he moved to Washington, Koop still frequently referred to Philadelphia as home.

Just two months after his arrival in Philadelphia, however, on December 7, 1941, the Japanese launched a sneak attack on the American fleet stationed at Pearl Harbor, Hawaii. The Japanese attack brought the United States into World War II and turned Koop's life upside down.

Pearl Harbor after the Japanese attack on December 7, 1941.

As millions of men were drafted and shipped overseas, so were thousands of doctors to care for the troops and the inevitable casualties. The drafting of doctors, however, caused a shortage here at home. As a result, many young interns such as Dr. Koop were called upon to perform work usually handled by more experienced doctors. Koop's two-year internship was halved, and his two-year lab job was canceled altogether. After just one year as an intern, Dr. C. Everett Koop began his surgical training.

Koop was ecstatic. Only five weeks into his surgical residency, Koop performed his first operation. His supervisor, Dr. Jeremy Rhoads, was involved in another surgery when an old woman came in needing an immediate gallbladder operation. Koop had watched the procedure many times, but he had never actually performed it himself. Koop was told to make the opening incision and then wait for Dr. Rhoads. But when Rhoads was delayed, Koop was forced to perform the surgery himself. Dr. Rhoads arrived just in time to watch Koop put in the final stitches.

Two days later, Dr. Rhoads called Koop into his office. "Chick, there is a patient who has just come into the emergency room with a bleeding ulcer. Would you go down and work him up and get him operated upon as soon as possible? . . . Call me only if you need me."[1] It was more than he could have hoped for. In just over a month, he was doing the work of a third-year resident.

Realizing his great opportunity, Koop threw himself unreservedly into his work. He often stayed at the hospital for days at a time, going home only to shower and change his clothes. It was a hard and demanding life that circumstances had thrust upon Chick Koop. For the next two years, he was on call for all 730 days and nights.

Eventually, this merciless schedule took its toll. Koop developed a peptic ulcer and became a patient himself. But even after his illness, Koop refused to slow down. "My happiest hours were those in the operating room," he recalled. "I felt called to live on the edge of the life-and-death decisions that need to be made there."[2]

Throughout this difficult time, Betty's support and devotion to her husband's career never wavered. She never once complained about the long hours or the financial hardships. As a resident, Koop earned only $1,000 a year, so again Betty had to take the primary responsibility for supporting them. Then in 1944, an additional responsibility was added—their first son, Allen, who was born in January.

On August 14, 1945—the day World War II ended—Betty and Allen were in Connecticut visiting her parents while Koop was still at the hospital, nursing two badly burned children in the emergency room. For the previous forty-eight hours he had kept a vigil at their bedsides. The second child had just died when the sirens sounded, signaling the Japanese surrender. People flooded into the streets around the hospital. They were shouting, whistling, and blowing horns. Even though it had been days since he last slept, Koop forgot his fatigue and joined the celebration, albeit with mixed emotions. He felt sadness for the two children and their families, but joy and relief that the war was finally over. He also felt uncertainty about his future.

Koop was nearing the end of his residency, and it was time to map out a career. He and Betty had planned to return to New York after Koop finished his training. But Koop had grown attached to Philadelphia and did not relish the prospect of leaving it. Then one day at five in the morning, Dr. Ravdin burst through the door to Koop's office.

"Chick, what do you plan to do with your life?" he asked. Koop told him that he had become quite fond of the University of Pennsylvania and wanted to stay on there. Koop suggested that he might take over the hospital's tumor clinic, which needed some guidance. But Ravdin had another idea, "How would you like to be surgeon-in-chief of the Children's Hospital instead?"[3]

The suggestion took Koop completely off guard. The field of pediatric surgery was not yet recognized as a separate specialty, and Koop, like most other doctors, knew very little about it. In fact, Koop had had virtually no training in pediatrics at all. In medical school, he had attended only six classes on the subject. And when his internship had been cut short because of the war, Koop missed his rotation in pediatrics altogether. As a surgical resident, he had rarely operated on children, and never on a newborn.

So why was a 29-year-old with no experience offered the job of chief of pediatric surgery? In part, it was because of Koop's natural talent as a surgeon. But he also got the job because no one else wanted it. Koop was actually Dr. Ravdin's fifth choice for the position; the previous four candidates had all turned him down. Koop would soon find out why.

After discussing it with Betty, Koop decided to accept Ravdin's offer. The plan was for him to spend three months at Children's Hospital, becoming acquainted with the facility, before moving to Boston to train at the Children's Hospital there. Finally, Koop would return to Philadelphia a year later and take over as surgeon-in-chief.

Koop was quite optimistic about his new position as he set off that first day for the Children's Hospital of Philadelphia, but his mood changed quickly once he arrived. Upon entering the hospital, Koop was immediately confronted by the chief medical resident. "Why don't you go back where you came from?" she snapped at him. "You're not needed here, you're not wanted here, and you put four good surgeons out of work."[4] It was not the greeting Koop had expected, but it set the tone for what lay ahead.

Koop received the same chilly reception everywhere he went at the hospital. The other doctors either ignored him or bluntly told him that he was unwelcome. Neither pediatricians nor general surgeons could understand the need for a specialty in children's surgery, and both groups resented the intrusion on their respective territories. As a final insult, instead of an office, Koop was given a small table in the corner of the hospital library, where he spent the next three months wondering whether he would ever be accepted there.

Two weeks before Koop's trial period was up, Betty gave birth to their second son, Norman. Then the Koop family moved to Boston for the next stage in Dr. Koop's pediatric training. At the Boston Children's Hospital, Koop would learn from the only two "child surgeons" in the country—Dr. William E. Ladd, the father of pediatric surgery, and his protégé, Dr. Robert E. Gross. These two men taught Koop the cardinal rule of pediatric surgery: You cannot treat children simply as small adults. Because children are physiologically different, they require special treatments and special procedures.

"Before pediatric surgeons developed techniques for surgery and post operative care, the way children suffered under surgery was almost criminal," Koop recalled.[5] Using adult techniques on children often caused terrible scarring and pain, unnecessarily lengthy recoveries, and sometimes even death. Koop was appalled. He returned to Children's Hospital in Philadelphia in November, 1946, determined to revolutionize the system of care there.

Koop had hoped that he would receive a warmer reception this time, but he was not so lucky. The doctors at Children's Hospital were just as hostile to him as they had been twelve months earlier. Even after his year of training in Boston, the doctors in Philadelphia still felt they knew children's medicine better than he did. To be accepted, Koop would have to prove himself.

A few months later, Koop got his opportunity. A dispute had developed between him and one of the senior pediatricians at the hospital, a Dr. Rappaport, over the treatment of a young boy suffering complications from pneumonia. Koop thought the child required surgery, but Dr. Rappaport insisted that surgery was unnecessary. Unable to resolve the issue themselves, the two doctors decided to present the case to their colleagues. This time, the other doctors backed Koop's diagnosis. It was the first time he had gained the support of his fellow doctors, and it somehow turned the tide in his favor. "No fireworks went off," Koop later remembered, "but I noticed a change in attitude of the other physicians. . . . A victory was won that Friday afternoon. . .a victory for pediatric surgery."[6] It was the first of many such victories Koop would win in his career.

5

Child Surgeon

In his thirty-five years as a pediatric surgeon, Charles Everett Koop revolutionized the field, developing new surgical techniques for children and perfecting existing ones. He took thousands of children whose cases had once been considered terminal and gave them the gift of a full, productive life. He may not have been the father of pediatric surgery, but Dr. Koop was certainly one of its greatest pioneers.

One of Koop's earliest goals was to make anesthesia safe for newborns and small children. At the time, infants were given doses far too large for their tiny bodies to tolerate, and Koop realized that many children were dying on the operating table not from the surgery, but from the effects of the excessive anesthesia. After months of experimentation, Koop developed a technique whereby the anesthesia was released to the infant one drop at a time, so that the doctor could better control the dosage. As a result, the lives of many thousands of infants have been, and will continue to be, saved.

Next, Dr. Koop turned his attention to the surgical procedures themselves. The first one he tackled was the hernia operation, the single most common procedure in pediatric surgery. Doctors typically made a three- to four-inch incision, operated for over an hour, then stitched the child up, leaving a large, jagged scar "that made the poor child look like a toy football with thick laces."[1] The child would then be bedridden for over a week following the surgery and be kept under careful watch for another six weeks.

When Koop was training in Boston, however, he had learned how to perform this operation without causing such traumatic results. By using a much shorter incision and a technique called subcuticular stitching, Koop found out that he could greatly reduce the child's pain and scarring. Subcuticular stitches were placed in, but not through, the skin and then covered with a protective liquid plastic, so not even a bandage was necessary. Furthermore, young hernia patients operated on in this manner had to spend only one night in the hospital and then could return home with little or no restrictions on their activities. Koop performed 17,000 of these operations in his career, completing most of them in under six minutes!

Dr. Koop also made groundbreaking strides in treating children plagued by life-threatening birth defects. When Koop began as chief surgeon, few operative procedures existed, and 95 to 100 percent of the children born with these problems died. But during his tenure at Children's Hospital, Koop developed and perfected new surgical cures for many of these once-fatal defects. By the time he retired from pediatric surgery, the mortality rate for infants with these problems had dropped to only 5 percent.

One of Koop's great successes came in the treatment of esophageal atresia. In this life-threatening but correctable condition, a child's esophagus—the tube that carries food from the throat to the stomach—is not connected to his or her stomach. When Koop began at Children's Hospital, virtually all children born with this condition died. In response, Koop developed an operative procedure to reattach the esophagus to the stomach, making this once-fatal problem almost entirely curable. By the end of his surgical career, Koop had performed 475 such operations and rarely lost a patient.

Dr. Koop also developed procedures to save children from countless other terminal or disfiguring defects—including hydrocephalus, otherwise known as "water on the brain," and diaphragmatic hernias, which occur when a child's abdominal organs invade the chest because of a hole in the child's diaphragm. One of these diaphragm operations still stands out in Koop's memory. One day, he received a frantic telephone call from a nearby hospital describing a sick newborn's condition. Immediately Koop recognized the symptoms of a diaphragmatic hernia. He jumped up, ran out of Children's Hospital, raced eleven blocks, and sprinted up nine flights of stairs to find the boy blue and lifeless.

Without waiting, Koop slashed open the child's chest cavity and pulled out the abdominal organs that were blocking his heart and lungs. Then he massaged the tiny newborn's heart and brought the child back to life. The infant was only fifty-five minutes old when Koop operated on him; it was the youngest patient of his career. About twenty-five years later, a tall, healthy-looking young man strode into Koop's office. "My father thought you'd like to meet me," the young man said. "You operated on me when I was fifty-five minutes old."[2] Not knowing what to say, Koop ran out from behind his desk and hugged his former patient. Although he operated on tens of thousands of children in his career, Dr. Koop quickly became as well-known for his compassion as he was for his skill. Koop frequently stayed up all night at the bedsides of ailing children and spent hours comforting frantic parents.

All the time spent with his patients, however, meant less time for Betty and their own children—Allen; Norman; David, born in 1947; and Betsy, born in 1951. Most days and nights, Koop's demanding schedule kept him at the hospital. But Betty had always known that her husband's career came

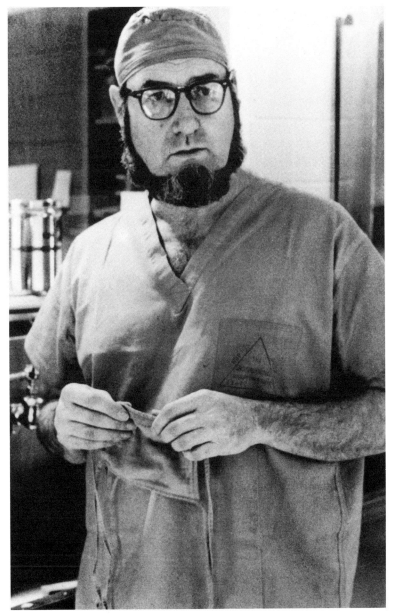

Dr. Koop leaves the operating room after performing surgery.

first, and she made sure their children never felt neglected. She assured them that their father would rather be home, but that he had to be at work so that he could save another child. As Allen Koop later recalled, "Although Dad was away a lot, Mom never let us feel he was absent from us."[3]

Because it was so rare, the time the Koop family spent together became all the more valuable. Chick Koop always tried to make it home for dinner, even if he had to return to the hospital later that night. And no matter how busy he was the rest of the year, he always reserved four to five weeks every summer to vacation with his family. From the last Friday in July through Labor Day, the Koops spent every summer in an old converted barn in Koop's favorite place—Hanover, New Hampshire. It was the one time of the year when Koop's professional life did not intrude on his personal life, and the family treasured it.

As their father had before them, the Koop children all became very attached to the New Hampshire countryside. David even decided to attend college there, following in his father's footsteps at Dartmouth. And just like Chick, David spent most of his free time in the mountains. He particularly enjoyed rock climbing, and most weekends he and his friends could be found scaling one of the granite peaks of New Hampshire's White Mountains.

One Sunday evening in the spring of 1968, the Koops were sitting at home waiting for their weekly call from David when the phone rang. But the voice on the other end of the line wasn't David's. It was the dean of Dartmouth College calling with tragic news. Earlier that day, David had gone with a friend to climb Cannon Mountain. The two were about halfway up the cliff face, and David was hammering in a piton, when a large section of the cliff broke off and carried

David with it. David fell 110 feet before his rope went taut and crashed him into the mountain. When his friend reached him, he found that David's left leg had been crushed and was bleeding profusely. The friend tried to stop the bleeding with a tourniquet, but the injury was too severe, and within ten minutes, David was dead.

In the weeks that followed, his father's grief was all-consuming. At work, Chick Koop became so emotional talking to the parents of dying children that he would have to cut the discussions short. "A doctor must never cry," he told Betty. "You're wrong," she said. "Now you can fully empathize."[4]

The Koops relied on their love for one another to carry them through the tragedy, though at times they turned to writing as a means to cope with their pain. The result was a book called *Sometimes Mountains Move*, which the family hoped might help others facing a similar loss. Chick Koop also relied on his religious faith to see him through.

He had always considered himself a Christian, having grown up in a church-going family, but Koop had not always been so devout. Early in his medical career, however, confronted with the daily pain and suffering of his tiny defenseless patients, Koop began to reexamine his religious faith. One Sunday, after finishing his morning rounds, Koop found himself outside the Tenth Presbyterian Church, a few blocks from the hospital. He quietly crept in the back door and went up to the balcony.

He had just dropped in for a look, but he soon found himself drawn into the sermon. In fact, Koop found the service so compelling that he returned the next Sunday morning and went back again, only a few hours later, for the evening service. Koop realized then that he was no simple observer; he was a believer.

From then on, Koop carried this faith with him every time he entered an operating room, believing that despite his technical skill, both he and his patient were in God's hands. Outside the operating room, Koop began praying at the bedsides of sick and dying children. This practice shocked his colleagues, many of whom felt he should keep his practice of religion separate from his practice of medicine. "As a person whose training and experiences put full faith in science, I came to see an even higher truth," Koop countered. "I saw a coexistence between science and God."[5]

Koop's spiritual awakening deeply affected all of his views and beliefs, public and private. It especially affected his views on the issue of abortion. In 1973, the Supreme Court concluded in the case of *Roe v. Wade* that women did indeed have the right to an abortion. The justices ruled that the right to privacy guaranteed by the Ninth Amendment encompassed the right of women to control their own bodies, even if that meant terminating a pregnancy. Koop strongly opposed the decision, believing that abortion was murder. Koop's Christian faith led him to believe that all life was sacred and ought to be protected, even the life of an unborn fetus. But Koop's opposition to abortion was not simply a result of his faith; it was also a response to his work.

After laboring for thirty-five years to save the lives of critically ill newborns, Dr. Koop could not accept the killing of fetuses only a few months younger. "My concern for the unborn followed as the night the day my concern about the newly born," Koop explained. "How could I ever accept the destruction of the unborn after a career devoted to the repair of imperfect newborns?"[6] He also feared the practice of abortion might be extended to include the killing of newborns with birth defects, and beyond that perhaps to the elimina-

Chick Koop with his wife, Betty, at a reception in his honor.

tion of all undesirable members of society—the old, the handicapped, and so on. Thinking as he did, Koop believed it was his moral responsibility to speak out publicly against abortion. And only six months after the decision in *Roe v. Wade* was announced, Dr. Koop did just that in a commencement address at Wheaton College, a religious school in Illinois. It was his first public statement against abortion, but it would certainly not be his last.

Over the next few years Koop made numerous public appearances all over the country speaking out against abortion. In 1976, he wrote *The Right to Live, The Right to Die*, in which he described his fear of abortion expanding to the killing of other unwanted people. The book sold more than 200,000 copies, and it established Koop's national reputation as an anti-abortion activist.

Then, the following year, Koop performed an operation that brought him even more national attention. The case involved a pair of Siamese twins who shared one and a half hearts. Koop had already successfully separated several pairs of Siamese twins, but none of those operations had been as tricky as this one promised to be. The twins were dying because their one, six-chambered heart wasn't large enough to support two growing bodies. The problem was that there was no way to separate the heart and save them both. The only option seemed to be to sacrifice one to save the other. After eleven days of painful consideration, Koop, in consultation with his colleagues and the family, decided that the stronger, larger twin would have the better chance of survival, and therefore was the one who should be saved.

The operation made history, as Koop became the first surgeon to successfully separate Siamese twins joined at the heart. His achievement made headlines in newspapers and magazines, and he was interviewed on television stations all over the country. Koop had always been well known within his profession, but now with his anti-abortion activities and this successful separation, he was becoming famous outside the medical community. And as his fame grew, Dr. Koop spent more and more time assailing abortion. During a program at York University in Toronto, Koop met Francis Schaeffer, a minister who was also delivering an anti-abortion lecture. After listening to each other speak, the two men decided to collaborate on an anti-abortion project entitled "What Ever Happened to the Human Race?" As it developed, the project grew to include five films, a book, and an extensive series of lectures and seminars.

From the fall of 1979 until his appointment as Surgeon General a year and a half later, Koop spent more time leading anti-abortion seminars around the country than practicing medicine. He delegated many of his responsibilities at the hospital, and though he continued to perform surgery, he referred cases involving long-term care to other doctors. Spending as much time as he did on the road, Dr. Koop quickly became one of the best known and most respected opponents of abortion. His activities eventually brought him to the attention of the Reagan campaign.

Koop testifies before the Senate during his confirmation hearings.

6

The Appointment Controversy

"For the first fifty years of my life," Charles Everett Koop once wrote, "abortion was a word I rarely heard. And when people talked about abortion, they usually whispered. The American society in which I grew up, and the American medical community which I joined fifty years ago, stood firmly against abortion. The consensus was clear: The fetus was an unborn child; abortion took a human life. Abortion was illegal because abortion was immoral. All that changed with dramatic speed. . . . Abortion has become not only a subject of everyday conversation and everyday practice, but also the most divisive public issue in American history since slavery."[1]

That division between pro-choice and anti-abortion forces was evident once again in the deluge of protests and demonstrations of support that Reagan's nomination of Dr. Koop as Surgeon General. Fearing that he would work to eliminate their right to an abortion if he became Surgeon General, pro-choice and women's groups such as Planned Parenthood and the National Organization for Women took out ads in the media and lobbied senators to vote against his confirmation.

Koop also received vehement opposition from a number of leading medical organizations, including the American Medical Association (AMA), the largest association of doctors in the country, and the American Public Health Association (APHA). The AMA had recently reversed its position on

Pro-choice activists march through the streets of Washington.

abortion, now favoring the woman's right to choose, while
the APHA had been pro-choice even before *Roe v. Wade*. Both
organizations wanted to distance themselves from Koop and
his anti-abortion beliefs. The APHA denounced Koop immediately, calling him, despite his forty years in medicine, "almost uniquely unqualified" to become Surgeon General.[2]

Soon the media latched on to the story, and the unmis-
takable visage of C. Everett Koop stared out at America from
newspapers, magazines, and televisions. It seemed that not a
day went by without a newspaper article or cartoon attacking
Koop's personal views or his professional competence. And
as though these repeated assaults weren't enough to endure,
Koop learned soon after his arrival in Washington of another
problem—a minor technicality, actually, the White House told
him. It seemed that according to an old, obscure law, the Surgeon General could not be older than 64 years and 29 days, so
technically, Dr. Koop was about a hundred days too old for

the job. Koop could still serve, of course, but before he could be confirmed, both houses of Congress would first have to vote to waive the age requirement.

Reagan's aides, of course, told Koop not to worry. After all, they said, many of the senators and congressmen themselves were older than Koop. How could they claim he was too old, when the Speaker of the House of Representatives himself was over 68 years old? But this technicality turned out to be a much bigger obstacle than Koop had been led to believe. Democrats in the House who opposed Koop's nomination on political grounds saw the issue of Koop's age as an opportunity to delay his confirmation while the opposition to Koop grew. As a result, the vote on the age waiver was held up for months until finally, after eighteen weeks of haggling, the House and Senate voted to waive the age requirement and accept his nomination.

After the vote, Koop relaxed, believing that the worst was over. Now that his nomination was solely in the hands of the Republican-controlled Senate, he expected a speedy and smooth confirmation. He was not alone in his assessment of the situation. As one newspaper columnist wrote, "With a Republican Senate, if Ronald Reagan wanted Jack the Ripper for Surgeon General, he'd get him confirmed."[3] The confirmation hearings began on October 1, 1981, and for the next two weeks, Koop watched as a parade of supporters and detractors praised and attacked him.

During the nine months leading up to his confirmation hearings, Koop had experienced an isolation unlike any he had ever known before, worse even than his initial experience at Children's Hospital. Reagan had appointed Koop to serve as deputy assistant secretary for health until his confirmation as Surgeon General came through. A letter from the

White House instructed Dr. Koop to report to an office on the seventh floor of the Department of Health and Human Services' Humphrey Building beginning March 9, 1981. When he got to his office, he found a large and starkly empty room, furnished only with a desk, a single chair, and a telephone.

On his first day, Dr. Koop sat silently behind his desk for eight hours. When he went down to the cafeteria for lunch, people stared at him and whispered, but no one approached him or talked to him. "My first day on the job. . .I felt worse than when I was a little boy on the first day at a new school," Koop recalled.[4] And his isolation continued for many months. Koop reported to work every day, but he had nothing to do. Through this difficult time, Koop later pointed out, he received not one word of encouragement from the White House. Most of the time, he sat at his giant oak desk and stared at the majestic dome of the Capitol building, wondering what he had done to deserve this treatment. "I couldn't understand," Koop wrote, "why God would disrupt such a peaceful, quiet, productive life, and bring me down into that mess."[5]

Paul Brand, a friend and fellow surgeon, visited Koop at the time. "I had the impression of a caged lion, full of enormous power," Brand recalled. "He paced the room, literally having nothing to do. And I also had the impression of a wounded man, a man in need of comfort."[6]

Dr. Koop's isolation and frustration became so severe at times that he considered withdrawing his name altogether. In fact, one day in late April, after weeks of being criticized by the press and political groups and ignored by his colleagues, Koop decided that he had finally had enough. He walked through the door of his one-room apartment that day to find Betty sitting on the couch with tears streaming down her

Koop talks to Arlen Specter of Pennsylvania (center) and Orrin Hatch of Utah (right), two of his supporters in the Senate.

cheeks. One look at the newspaper on her lap told Chick why she was crying. The headline in the *Washington Post* read "Dr. Kook."

"I don't need this!" Koop exclaimed, crumpling the newspaper and throwing it on the floor. "I've never been treated this way before, and it's wrong to put my family through it now." It was Betty, however, his greatest supporter, who refused to let him give up. "If you quit now, you'll always wonder," she told him. "And don't forget—you no longer have a job in Philadelphia."[7]

Finally, Chick Koop realized that he couldn't quit because he was on a mission. In those months alone in his office in the

Humphrey building, Koop had found plenty of time to think about the position of Surgeon General and the opportunities that it offered to inform people and to save lives. Later, Dr. Koop would look back on that difficult time as a remarkable gift. "I had a chance to look at the health problems of the nation and wonder what I could do about them when I was finally let loose. I decided I would use the office to espouse the cause of the disenfranchised: handicapped children, the elderly, people in need of organ transplantation, women and children who were being battered and abused. During that nine months, I developed a detailed agenda, something no Surgeon General has ever had before. In the end, that period of acute frustration made possible every single thing I was able to accomplish in office."[8]

On November 16, 1981, the Senate, by a vote of 68 to 24, finally confirmed Dr. C. Everett Koop as Surgeon General of the United States. He was sworn in quietly and immediately.

7

Baby Doe

With Koop's confirmation, the Reagan administration hoped to put the controversial appointment behind it. Koop himself had no desire to remain so prominently in the public eye. Yet Dr. Koop continued to attract attention, beginning innocently enough with his surprising decision to wear the official military uniform of the Surgeon General.

It had been decades since a Surgeon General had put on the traditional uniform of the office—a starched blue costume with three-starred epaulets and gold braids. But Koop insisted on wearing his, believing that the uniform would lend authority to an office that had been so seriously weakened. He hoped the uniform might also help raise the morale of the Public Health Service, which was at an all-time low following President Reagan's decision to slash 2,600 staff jobs in order to save money. The officers of the Public Health Service who remained were left feeling undervalued and neglected. In an unfortunately misguided attempt to raise their spirits, Koop urged his colleagues to join him in wearing the traditional dress.

Immediately, there were complaints, not the least of which pointed to the cost of buying and maintaining such a uniform. Then there were problems with the look of the uniform itself. More than once, airplane passengers mistook Koop for a steward and asked him to help with their luggage. But Koop saw nothing comic about the uniform, and he continued to wear it without apology.

Political cartoonists, always looking for something new to poke fun at, cherished Koop and his stubborn lack of self-consciousness, devoting some of their best work to the new Surgeon General. Who is this man, they asked, with the Abraham Lincoln beard and the uniform from "The Love Boat?" After all, this six-foot-one, 210-pound man in the uniform of a three-star admiral was a very memorable and striking figure. Yet Koop easily withstood these efforts to portray him as a laughable character. He had learned during his confirmation hearings to ignore the press and get on with his work. Barely five months after Koop assumed office, however, just when the uniform controversy had finally been laid to rest, the Surgeon General again found himself back in the news. The case involved a baby who had been born with a serious birth defect and potentially fatal complications. What made this case different, however, was that the parents had decided to refuse treatment for their child.

On April 9, 1982, a woman living in Bloomington, Indiana, had given birth to a child suffering from Down's syndrome, a disease that would certainly leave the infant severely mentally retarded. This alone was not life-threatening. But the child suffered from additional complications, including esophageal atresia, that would prove fatal if they remained untreated. Dr. Owens, who had delivered their baby, told the couple that their child would have only a 50 percent chance of surviving surgery, and even if the baby did survive, there was no hope of its ever becoming a functioning person. Two other physicians, a pediatrician and the family doctor, both strongly disagreed and recommended immediate surgery. In the end, the parents took the advice of Dr. Owens and allowed the child—dubbed "Baby Doe" by the press—to die what they referred to as a "natural death."

When the Surgeon General heard about the case, he tried to override the parents' wishes. As Koop well knew, having pioneered the procedure, esophageal atresia could easily be corrected with surgery. In his career, he had operated on hundreds of children with this problem, with an ever-increasing rate of success. He admitted that nothing could be done about the Down's syndrome and its resulting retardation, but the esophagus could still be repaired and the infant could live. All his life, Koop had worked long hours to save the lives of children with similar problems. To his mind, there was nothing to debate. Regarding the question of whether or not to keep alive a child incapable of making its own desires known, the answer was clear. Koop announced to the country that withholding treatment was nothing less than murder.

Koop's stand on the Baby Doe evoked a panoply of public reaction. Many people accused him of acting merely on his personal religious beliefs. They believed Koop's stance on the Baby Doe case, like his stance on abortion, was motivated solely by his Christian faith. But as with the abortion issue, this conclusion was only partially true. Koop's feelings regarding the case were affected by his religious belief in the sanctity of life, but they were just as much the product of his sense of responsibility as a public health officer and his medical commitment to the preservation of life.

Others strongly supported Koop's attempt to obtain treatment for Baby Doe, including the nursing staff at the Bloomington hospital. Anti-abortion groups added to the furor with protests denouncing the parents as "murderers." Several families publicly offered to adopt the child. An Indiana judge, however, ruled in favor of the parent's right to take the advice of their chosen physician, and six days after its birth, the baby died.

During those six days, the Baby Doe case was the top news story in the country, and every American seemed to have an opinion. After the child died, some contributed to a public outcry against what they saw as the willful killing of a helpless baby. People wrote letters to their congressmen demanding legislation that would prevent such injustices in the future. And then, incredibly, just a few months later, there was a second case, "Baby Jane Doe," involving a baby girl who had been born on Long Island with severe complications. The infant was diagnosed as having spina bifida, a spinal disease that can cause both mental retardation and a fatal infection if not treated immediately.

As in the first case, the parents favored withholding treatment and allowing the baby to die a natural death. And again Koop opposed their decision. This time, the Surgeon General tried to subpoena the baby's medical records, claiming that the doctors in charge had a "medical imperative" to treat the infection. He also took his campaign to the media. "We're not just fighting for this baby," Koop proclaimed during a television interview on "Face The Nation." "We're fighting for the principle of this country that every life is individually and uniquely sacred."[1] But once again Dr. Koop was unsuccessful in forcing the parents to accept treatment for their child.

As a physician, Koop believed that doctors were better equipped than government bureaucrats to judge the best treatment for their patients. But he also wanted desperately to protect handicapped infants from unnecessary death, so he supported government intervention in those cases involving the withholding of care. The Justice Department agreed with Koop and pushed for the passage of strict codes regulating the exact course of action to be taken by doctors in these cases.

Koop often made public speaking appearances as Surgeon General.

Because the regulations restricted a doctor's right to treat a patient as he or she saw fit, however, they were overturned by the courts.

Strangely enough, Koop was not upset by the successful challenges to the Baby Doe regulations. Although he wanted more than anything to prevent future Baby Doe deaths, he believed that the course of treatment had to be decided on a case-by-case basis. Because no two cases were alike, the Justice Department's plan was much too rigid. Instead, Koop decided to draft his own plan. He also decided that, in the process, he would interview people on both sides of the Baby Doe issue, those who wanted government regulations as well as those who wanted physicians and parents to decide.

The difference between the conservative and liberal approaches was immediately obvious. Anti-abortion conservatives demanded ironclad government regulations that would allow the government to compel treatment, even against the parents' wishes. Liberals, on the other hand, opposed government intervention, believing the choice should be left to the individuals involved. So, too, did organizations such as the American Pediatrics Association, which opposed government intervention on the grounds that it would remove families and their doctors from the decision-making process. Koop considered both of these arguments carefully and decided to forge a compromise as best he could. The Surgeon General's plan called for the establishment of patient-care review committees within local hospitals. These committees— made up of ten to fifteen hospital and community leaders— would consult on the treatment in Baby Doe cases so that no individual alone would have the power to make a life-or-death decision.

Koop's plan was later struck down by the courts for many of the same reasons that the Justice Department's Baby Doe regulations were. But it nevertheless prompted action on Capitol Hill. In the summer of 1984, Congress overwhelmingly approved an amendment to the Child Abuse Act that defined the refusal to treat handicapped newborns as child abuse. Including Baby Doe cases under the umbrella of the Child Abuse Act allowed the federal government to withhold federal funds from states that refused to adopt guidelines guaranteeing the medical rights of disabled infants.

Though Koop did, in the end, support limited government intervention, the Surgeon General's actions on the Baby Doe issue forced liberals to question the assumptions they had made about the man. They began to see less of the stern patriarch who had already made up his mind and more of the public servant who might be open to other points of view. Could it be, they asked themselves, that we misjudged him? And conservatives also began to re-evaluate Koop. Radical anti-abortionists considered his patient-care committees a surrender to the medical establishment, interpreting Koop's willingness to compromise as the first sign that he might not be as dependable as they had believed.

Ultimately, their feeling of disappointment matched his own. As disillusioned as anti-abortionists were by Koop's willingness to compromise, Koop himself was frustrated by their all-or-nothing mentality. Although Koop's personal views remained unwavering, as Surgeon General he could see the value of legislative compromise, whereas right-wing groups that placed ideology above integrity could not. The Baby Doe issue opened a rift between Dr. Koop and his one-time allies that would continue to widen.

8

Putting the Heat on Tobacco Road

"A thousand people will stop smoking today. Their funerals will be held sometime during the next three or four days."[1] This was how C. Everett Koop began his lectures on the health effects of smoking. And in his eight years as Surgeon General, Dr. Koop gave many such lectures.

No single health issue absorbed more of Koop's time or energy than smoking, the leading cause of preventable death in the United States. As Surgeon General, Dr. Koop led the strongest anti-smoking campaign in American history. This meant taking on the fearsome tobacco industry, which had long possessed one of the most powerful lobbies in American politics. It was also a group that had, during his confirmation, encompassed some of Koop's strongest supporters.

Koop had always vehemently opposed smoking. As a young man, he had worried about his father's habit, and as he grew older, his opposition stiffened. Yet, despite his personal aversion to smoking, Koop did not accept the post of Surgeon General with an anti-smoking crusade in mind. It was not until he studied tobacco's deadly effects during his term in office that Dr. Koop became determined to campaign against this silent killer. Studies had shown conclusively that smoking led to cancer of the lung, mouth, esophagus, stomach, and bladder, as well as heart disease, stroke, and emphysema. In 1981, the year Koop became Surgeon General, smoking caused the deaths of more than 400,000 Americans, one sixth of all the deaths in the country and more than those caused by alcohol, drugs, automobile accidents, and AIDS combined. The figures proved that smoking was, by far, the single greatest threat to the nation's health. And as the nation's chief health official, Dr. Koop knew it was his responsibility to do something about it.

Koop was not the first Surgeon General to inform Americans about the dangers of tobacco. Almost twenty years before, on January 11, 1964, Luthur Terry had issued the first Surgeon General's report on smoking. The report documented higher mortality rates in smokers than non-smokers and prompted Congress to pass a law requiring cigarette companies to use the warning label: "Caution: Cigarette Smoking May Be Hazardous to Your Health."

Terry's groundbreaking report shocked the American public.

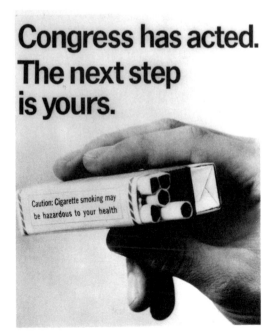

Congress has acted. The next step is yours.

Caution: Cigarette smoking may be hazardous to your health

An American Cancer Society poster.

At the time, most people saw smoking as just one more recreational activity—one that made you look sophisticated while you did it. Even among doctors, few imagined it might be a health hazard. In 1964, over half of the adult population in the United States smoked. But Terry's report made a difference. Americans became generally more health conscious during the late 1960s and 1970s, and the early 1980s saw a glut of health crazes from diets to aerobics classes. People watched their cholesterol intake and their salt intake, and many quit smoking. Twenty years earlier, smoking had been considered chic and sophisticated, but a generation later, it was seen by many as a bad, unhealthful habit. Still, in 1981, 33 percent of the adult population smoked cigarettes.

In 1982, Koop issued his own *Surgeon General's Report on Smoking and Health*. It was the most serious indictment of smoking ever made by the Public Health Service, announcing that smoking was responsible for 30 percent of all cancer deaths in the United States. The following year, Koop produced another report in which he declared that smoking caused even more deaths from heart disease than from cancer. The 1984 report proved to be the most important, however, coming as it did on the twentieth anniversary of Luthur Terry's original broadside. In addition to his regular annual report, Koop decided to commemorate the anniversary with an additional anti-smoking effort.

Koop's goal was to wipe out smoking entirely in the United States. But with a small budget and no real authority, the Surgeon General couldn't ban smoking himself. Dr. Koop would have to get Americans to quit smoking voluntarily, so he decided to center his 1984 anniversary speech around a call for a "Smoke-Free Society by the Year 2000." Koop was scheduled to deliver the address in Miami before the American Lung Association that May. Chick Koop had been giving speeches for more than four decades, but he had never worked as hard or as long on a speech as he did on this one. Furthermore, Koop was very careful to keep the content of the speech a secret. He worried that allies of the tobacco industry, including many highly placed members of the Reagan administration, would try to suppress the speech if they knew what it contained. Dr. Koop was determined not to allow political pressure to stand in the way of saving lives.

In his speech, Koop appealed to smokers to give up the habit for their own benefit. He also admonished non-smokers to stand up for the right to live and work in a smoke-free environment. There was no reason, he said, that non-smokers should tolerate smoking if it offended them. "By the end of the century," Koop said, "the attitudes of the American public should evolve to the point where no smoker will light up in the presence of a non-smoker without having first secured permission to do so."[2]

Then Koop proclaimed that his report was only the first step in a nationwide campaign—the "SFS-2000" campaign—that would carry the message all around the country. Everyone from the Boy Scouts to the American Association of Retired Persons would hear about the dangers of smoking. Immediately following his lecture in Miami, Koop launched a nationwide tour to present his "Smoke-Free Society" campaign.

As he had expected, Koop's "SFS-2000" campaign infuriated many of his conservative allies, including Senator Jesse Helms from the tobacco growing state of North Carolina. Helms had been one of the Surgeon General's staunchest supporters during his confirmation, but now he called for Koop's resignation. Koop's campaign also outraged President Reagan, who had long been a friend of the tobacco industry. In

A young student from the Smoke-Free Class of 2000.

his 1980 presidential campaign, for instance, Reagan had promised to "end what has become an increasingly antagonistic relationship between the federal government and the tobacco industry."[3] In fact, the president personally guaranteed that "my own cabinet members will be far too busy with substantive matters to waste their time proselytizing against the dangers of cigarette smoking."[4] Now that a member of his own administration was doing just that, Ronald Reagan was determined to put a stop to it.

The White House tried every way it could, short of firing Koop, to derail the Surgeon General's anti-smoking campaign. Early on, Koop faced off with Defense Secretary Caspar Weinberger over the issue of cigarette discounts for military personnel. The policy of offering cigarettes at substantial discounts had begun during World War II, when the number of smokers in the United States increased dramatically as soldiers, sailors, and marines all took advantage of the cheap prices. When Koop proposed banning these long-standing discounts, the Defense Department bluntly refused. Secretary Weinberger claimed he could not accept the ban because it was unfair. But there was much speculation that Weinberger's real reason for opposing the ban was the pressure he was feeling from the White House and the tobacco lobby.

Despite White House opposition, Koop lobbied against Weinberger's decision. "It just doesn't make sense to me," he said in a widely reported statement. "How could the removal of cigarettes be viewed as a reduction in benefits when the only benefits of smoking are a lifetime of illness and an early death?"[5]

Again in 1986, the Surgeon General clashed with the administration over smoking. This time, the specific issue was cigarette advertising. Congress had already banned cigarette ads on radio and television, and now it was debating whether or not to outlaw cigarette ads in newspapers and magazines and on billboards as well. Officially, the Reagan administration opposed the bill, responding once again to pressure from the tobacco industry. But the Reagan aides charged with burying the bill had one problem—the Surgeon General had been called to testify before Congress, and they knew he would speak in favor of the bill. To keep Koop quiet, the White House chief of staff, Donald Regan, decided to stop Koop from testifying. Regan's plan backfired, however, when the press learned of his attempts to block Koop's testimony. So instead of silencing the Surgeon General's anti-smoking message, the White House made it front-page news.

To allay the scandal, Regan relented and allowed Koop to testify, but only with an official of the Justice Department at his side to give the White House view. Testifying first, the Justice Department spokesman told the committee that the administration had "very serious concerns" about banning advertising of any kind, and that it was "not convinced that the case had been made that cigarette advertising leads to increased consumption."[6] Given his turn, Koop politely disagreed. Cigarette advertising, the Surgeon General said, "increases the total universe of users and increases consumption by those who already use it. It does this, and it does it effectively."[7] Why, he asked, would the tobacco industry spend $4,000 *per minute* on cigarette advertising if the ads didn't work?

Even worse, according to Koop, was the misleading way the ads presented smoking. "Many ads portray smoking as a safe, if not healthful activity," Koop said, "and no ads disclose many of the serious and extensive health effects of smoking such as stroke and nicotine addiction."[8] Koop offered this example: "One of the more outrageous cigarette ads has, for at least a decade, used the slogan: `Alive with Plea-sure'. . .If you consider smokers who suffer from lung cancer or emphysema, truth in advertising would demand use of the slogan: `Dying in Agony.'"[9]

The bill was ultimately defeated, but Koop's anti-smok-ing message reached both the lawmakers and the public, and during the next few years, Dr. Koop made great strides in convincing smokers to quit. All across the nation, restaurants, offices, movie theaters, and even airlines banned smoking, while other establishments limited the practice. By the time Koop left the Surgeon General's office, the percentage of smokers in the United States had dropped from one-third to one-quarter of the adult population.

9

AIDS

Just as the dust was settling from the debate over cigarette advertising, a new crisis gripped the office of the Surgeon General. Smoking was a long-term problem requiring a long-term solution. What the Surgeon General now faced, however, was an immediate emergency that many predicted would, sooner rather than later, explode into the greatest public health catastrophe of the century. The object of this concern was an obscure disease called acquired immune deficiency syndrome. Soon, it became popularly know by its initials: AIDS.

When C. Everett Koop first came to Washington in 1981, most people had never heard of AIDS, doctors included. Not until June of that year did a report from the Centers for Disease Control (CDC) in Atlanta bring the illness to the attention of the medical community. The CDC report discussed the cases of five previously healthy homosexual men now suffering from the same rare strain of pneumonia. A month later, the CDC reported the cases of twenty-six gay men who had contracted yet another rare virus. The CDC investigated these and other unusual cases involving gay men and discovered that they all had something in common. Each of the men involved, who were otherwise healthy, had contracted a virus that was defeating their natural capacity to resist disease. The AIDS virus itself wasn't killing them, but it was destroying their bodies' ability to fight other potentially fatal diseases, such as pneumonia.

The medical community was baffled. No one could identify the AIDS virus or even figure out how people were getting it. All the doctors knew was that AIDS was deadly and that it was spreading quickly. By August, the CDC had already reported 108 confirmed cases of AIDS. Of these people, forty-three had already died. And during the next two years, AIDS spread even faster into a nationwide epidemic, killing thousands of people. Soon the media became interested, and by 1985, most educated people knew about the tens of thousands of Americans dying of AIDS. Still, it took the AIDS-related death that summer of movie star Rock Hudson to push the epidemic onto the front pages. Soon everyone everywhere was talking about AIDS—everyone, that is, except the president and his administration.

Reagan administration officials had known about AIDS ever since its discovery in 1981, but the president had intentionally ignored the issue. Even as the public focus on AIDS intensified, the president continued to avoid the subject. The reason had a lot to do with the groups of people most affected by the disease. Initially, most AIDS patients were either homosexual men, who often engaged in unsafe sexual practices, or intravenous drug users, who regularly used contaminated needles to shoot the drugs into their veins. Because President Reagan believed that both homosexuality and intravenous drug use were immoral, he tended to see AIDS as God's way of punishing this behavior.

Many other conservatives shared this moralistic viewpoint, chief among them the White House communications director, Patrick Buchanan, and Reagan's top domestic policy advisor, Gary Bauer. These extremely influential men both considered AIDS to be divine revenge against unrepentant sinners. "The silver lining in this tragic situation," Bauer said, "is that it may get people. . .to behave. . . . There is nothing like the threat of death to get the glands under control."[1]

Under the influence of Buchanan and Bauer, and in keeping with the president's own feelings, the Reagan administration adopted a policy of silence on the issue of AIDS, believing that "God's judgment should be allowed to run its course."[2] And this policy extended most specifically to the office of the Surgeon General. Because the Surgeon General was a member of the executive branch, responsible to the Department of Health and Human Services, he had to obey his superiors. His immediate boss during Reagan's first term was Assistant Secretary Edward Brandt, who shared the president's belief that AIDS was God's plague against sin. In keeping with White House policy as well as his and Reagan's own personal views, Brandt ordered Koop not to talk about the epidemic. Whenever Koop appeared on a talk show or at a press conference, Brandt's office insisted that reporters refrain from asking questions about AIDS. And when Brandt created an executive task force to explore the AIDS issue in 1983, he refused to let Koop join it.

In this manner, the Reagan administration put off having to address the AIDS crisis for nearly six years. As late as 1986, the president still avoided any explicit discussion of the disease that had already claimed more than ten thousand lives. As public pressure mounted, however, the president realized he would have to act. So on February 5, 1986, President Reagan finally ordered his Surgeon General to prepare a report on the epidemic. It had taken over five years for the president to decide that the nation's chief health officer should address the nation's most pressing health threat. But once Dr. Koop's hands were untied, he worked furiously to make up for the lost time. For the next two years, C. Everett Koop let the AIDS crisis take over his life. The job of the Surgeon General is to educate the American public about the prevention of disease and the promotion of health. "I realized that if ever there was a disease made for a Surgeon General, it was AIDS," Koop later said.[3]

By this time, the country was beginning to panic. People knew AIDS was deadly, but few really understood how one got the disease or how to protect themselves. Many people feared that just being near someone who had AIDS, or touching them, could make them catch it. People who knew little or nothing about the disease began calling for quarantines of AIDS patients, and reports of discrimination against homo-

Frightened parents protest to keep AIDS patients out of schools.

sexuals skyrocketed. Gay rights leaders and other AIDS groups feared a witch-hunt.

Koop knew that these injustices would continue until people were told the truth about AIDS. By this time, researchers had identified the virus that caused AIDS and had even given it a name: the human immunodeficiency virus (HIV). Even more importantly, though, they had discovered how the HIV virus was transmitted. Contrary to popular belief, AIDS could not be spread through such casual contact as touching an infected person or drinking from the same glass. It turned out that the HIV virus could be passed on only through sexual intercourse, through the use of a contaminated needle, through the umbilical cord of an AIDS-infected mother, or through the transfusion of contaminated blood.

Even before it was written, Koop's report sparked controversy. Liberal activists repeatedly questioned the Surgeon General's willingness to be open-minded in dealing with AIDS. After all, Koop's views on homosexuality were well known. Gay rights groups were therefore openly cynical about Dr. Koop's ability to consider the matter objectively. They assumed that Koop's report would inevitably support the Reagan administration's conclusion that AIDS victims deserved their disease. Conservatives, too, believed that Koop's religious views would color his report on AIDS. The radical right rested easy, confident that Koop's report would condemn homosexuality and other "sinful" behavior.

Koop, however, was determined not to allow his personal feelings about homosexuality to affect his professional judgment. He decided instead to use this report as a means to educate the public and correct the many prevailing misconceptions about AIDS. To get a balanced assessment of the issue, Koop once again decided to consult people on both sides. The Surgeon General spent months interviewing every-one from leaders of the National Coalition of Black Lesbians and Gays to radically conservative Christians as well as several medical experts on AIDS, including Dr. Anthony Fauci of the National Institutes of Health. Koop made sure that no group was denied a chance to express its views. "He listened very carefully, and didn't ask too many questions," Gary MacDonald, then executive director of the AIDS Action Council, recalled. "He gave me no sense of what he was thinking or what he planned to write in his report."[4]

During this time, Dr. Koop also made trips to nearby hospitals to meet with AIDS patients personally. "He would sit at the bedside of a young person with AIDS," according to one hospital official, "and inwardly question the practice of homosexuality, which seemed to contradict every one of his Christian family values. But then he'd look at the patient's sunken eyes and emaciated body, and be struck by how defenseless the boy seemed."[5] Many people close to Koop have said that he never did reexamine his basic, overall condemnation of homosexuality—this remained fixed. Instead, he simply understood that his duty as a public health officer required him not to judge people, but to protect their health. Koop himself explained it this way: "If an ambulance pulls up and unloads two wounded men, a bank robber who shot a guard and the bank guard who returned fire, which man does the doctor treat first? The doctor must go with the most urgent wounds, not the most moral one."[6]

"I still view the [homosexual] lifestyle with a certain revulsion," Koop said. "But I am the Surgeon General of all the people: of the heterosexuals and the homosexuals, of the young and old, of the moral and immoral. I don't have the luxury of deciding which side I want to be on."[7]

Koop was concerned that the president might appoint a committee to review his report and thereby weaken it. So before agreeing to write the AIDS report, he demanded complete independence. "I'm not going to clear it with anybody before I deliver it to the White House," the Surgeon General announced. "I'm going to do a health report. . .and it's not going to be political."[8]

Koop took every precaution to prevent his report from being leaked to the press before it was finished. Instead of working at his office, where many more people would have access to the report, he wrote it at home at a desk in the basement of his rented home in Georgetown. He numbered each of his seventeen drafts so that he would know if any were missing. And when he finally finished the report on September 19, 1986, he hand-delivered it to the White House. Finally on October 22, 1986, Koop read the report to a packed press conference. "It's time to put self-defeating attitudes aside and recognize that we are fighting a disease and not a people," he said.[9]

In the report, Koop carefully outlined how the AIDS virus was transmitted—and how it was not. Then he went on to discuss how people could protect themselves. He told people not to share needles, and he spoke graphically and forthrightly about safe and unsafe sexual practices. Koop told his audience that the only way to be completely safe was to abstain from sex or have sex with only one, faithful, uninfected partner. But Koop didn't stop there. He went on to shock conservatives by recommending the use of condoms for people who had more than one sexual partner or who engaged in homosexual sex. And, disregarding Reagan administration policy entirely, he advocated an intensive program of sex education in the schools, beginning "at the earliest possible age," which he defined as the third grade. "Many people, especially our youth," Koop said, "are not receiving the information that is vital to their future health and well-being because of our reticence in dealing with the subjects of sex, sexual practices, and homosexuality. This silence must end."[10]

Liberals were stunned and delighted. The associate executive director of the American Public Health Association, Katherine McCarter, commended Koop for his courage, and Faye Wattleton, the president of Planned Parenthood, praised Koop for his "candor, accuracy, and lack of moralizing."[11] Jeffrey Levi, executive director of the National Gay and Lesbian Task Force said that "the bottom line on Koop is that it shows you never to give up on anyone, whether it's your parents, or the Surgeon General."[12]

Conservatives, on the other hand, were outraged and appalled at the Surgeon General's explicit language and his "acceptance" of homosexuality and promiscuity. "His report on AIDS looks and reads like it was edited by the Gay Task Force," conservative advocate Phyllis Schlafly said.[13] Especially upsetting to Koop's former supporters on the right was the report's emphasis on sex education, including its candid discussion of the effectiveness of condoms in protecting against transmission of the disease. For the Reagan administration, the use of the word *condom* itself caused great dismay. Some officials tried to convince Koop to remove the condom reference, but the doctor refused. "The White House doesn't like the C word," Koop said. "But if you don't talk about condoms, people are going to die. So I talk."[14]

Unable to keep Koop quiet, the Reagan White House launched its own campaign attacking the Surgeon General's condom recommendation. Secretary of Education William Bennett released his own report, "AIDS and the Education of

Children," in which he directly contradicted the Surgeon General. "Promoting the use of condoms," Bennett said, "can suggest to teenagers that adults expect them to engage in sexual intercourse."[15] White House domestic policy advisor Gary Bauer added, "I don't see why a third-grader needs to know anything about condoms or sexual practices." [16]

Both men echoed the conservative line that the only proper sexual advice for adolescents was abstinence. Personally, Koop shared their view that adolescents should not engage in any form of sexual intercourse. But he stuck to his public position. "Many young people—despite what their parents would like—have already become sexually active with one or more partners," Koop said. "And I think I'm a realist enough to know that when you take a 17-year-old boy who has begun to have sexual relationships, he is almost never going to turn around and go back to abstinence. This is the group that is not going to listen to a just-say-no program; so we have to say, `Unless you are absolutely certain about your partner—and how can you be?—you've got to protect yourself against AIDS.'"[17]

Eighteen months after its release, and over the strong objections of the White House, Congress approved a public mailing of Koop's report. In May of 1988, a simplified version of the AIDS report was sent to every household in the United States. The six-page booklet dealt with the symptoms, transmission, and prevention of AIDS. It also made a grim prediction: that 179,000 American would die of AIDS by 1991. This condensed version of the report along with Koop's own media campaign triggered a revolution in the public awareness of AIDS and other sexual issues. Before the Surgeon General's report was issued, the mass media rarely allowed discussions of condoms. But Dr. Koop's bluntly clinical report changed that. Within months, public service ads appeared in magazines promoting the use of condoms, and in April of 1988, the first condom ad appeared on national television. It featured a young woman who says, "I'll do a lot for love, but I'm not ready to die for it."

"The impact of the report was tremendous," Koop said a year after the mailing. "Six months ago, the controversy was `What are we going to do about this terrible problem of sex education?' Now the problem is `How soon can we get the state legislatures to make sure our kids learn something about their own sexuality?'"[18] Koop's public awareness campaign was indeed a tremendous success, but it cost him dearly with his former political allies among the conservatives. His relationship with influential members of the Reagan administration, already strained by his anti-smoking activities, deteriorated further still.

Koop speaks before the National Press Club in Washington.

10

"America's Family Doctor"

Late in March, 1987, Koop delivered a speech on the AIDS crisis to the National Press Club in Washington. Afterward, one of the reporters there asked the Surgeon General what advice he would give to a pregnant woman infected with the AIDS virus. Koop responded that he would never advise anyone to have an abortion, but that as an ethical physician, he would have to inform his patient of all her legal options—including abortion. Later Koop said that he realized immediately that he had answered the question too quickly, but it was too late. The next morning, his worst fears were realized. The headlines read: KOOP SUPPORTS ABORTION.

The Surgeon General's outspokenness on AIDS turned many of his conservative allies against him, but this new abortion controversy was another matter entirely. Before Koop had a chance to clarify his statement, impatient anti-abortion groups fired back. One of Koop's strongest supporters during his confirmation fight, conservative spokesperson Phyllis Schlafly, sounded their frustration: "In the last several months. . .Koop has been no friend. He has been promoting condoms as an effective measure against AIDS. . . . He has urged sex education at the lowest grade possible. . . . And now he has said that abortion is a legal option for pregnant women with AIDS."[1] Ironically, the same issue that had brought Koop into office was now heralding his exit. As Koop himself said, "As abortion dominated my first nine months in Washington, it also clouded my exit from government office."[2]

Ronald Reagan had campaigned during two elections on the promise that he would work tirelessly to outlaw abortion. But now, seven years after the first of those promises was made, anti-abortion conservatives had understandably lost much of their patience with the president and his administration. Near the end of his second and final term, President Reagan still had not taken decisive action on the abortion issue. Dr. Koop had been his sop to them, but that appointment hadn't worked out as planned. So with the intention of assuaging the anti-abortion forces, President Reagan asked his Surgeon General to write a report on the health effects of abortion. Reagan believed that such a report would show that abortion was a health threat to women, which might provide the Supreme Court with a basis for overturning the *Roe v. Wade* decision that had legalized abortion. For years, anti-abortion groups had charged that abortion was a dangerous surgical procedure that often led to future miscarriages, infertility, and sometimes even death. Furthermore, they argued that deciding to have an abortion was so stressful that women often suffered mental and emotional problems such as severe depression.

From the beginning, Koop was uncomfortable with the president's request. He knew that the White House's assumption that abortion was damaging to women's health was probably just wishful thinking, and he doubted there would be enough scientific evidence to support this conclusion. He asked the president to withdraw his request, but Koop was told that the president never changed his mind. So, reluctantly, Koop set to work.

As had become his habit, Koop began conducting interviews with medical experts as well as the leaders of various interest groups. He offered an open invitation to anyone who

Anti-abortion supporters rally in front of the Supreme Court.

wanted to make his or her views known and spoke with pro-choice and anti-abortion activists as well as women who shared with him their own personal experiences with abortion. It didn't take long for Koop to realize that little of the information he was receiving could be considered objective or scientific. He tried to uncover unbiased medical research on the subject, but every study he found reflected the opinion of the group or person writing it. By October, 1988, Koop had determined that, because there was no unbiased evidence, it would be impossible for him to reach a scientific conclusion either way. He decided to write a letter to the president explaining why he could not write the report.

But he wouldn't write just yet because the White House was in an uproar. President Reagan was about to leave office, and his staff was occupied tying up loose ends. Meanwhile, Vice-President George Bush was campaigning to replace Reagan, and the presidential election was only a month away. The Surgeon General realized that the time was not right to contact the president about his abortion report, so he decided to wait until after the election was over before writing his letter. Then on January 9, 1989, two months after Bush's victory, Koop drafted the letter, which read in part, "I regret, Mr. President, that. . .the effects of abortion simply cannot support either the preconceived notions of those pro-life or those pro-choice." "In spite of a diligent review," Koop continued, ". . .the scientific studies do not prove conclusive data about the health effects of abortion on women."[3]

Koop delivered the letter to the White House personally. He had hoped the president would see him, but instead Dr. Koop was met by an aide. Koop asked for and received a promise that the letter would not be released to the press until after the president had read it and responded. But when Chick Koop returned home, he found Betty waiting for him in the driveway with bad news. The television networks were already reporting, in a distorted version of Koop's letter, that "the Surgeon General could find no evidence that abortion is psychologically harmful" to women.[4] Koop spent the next several days trying to set the record straight, speaking to newspaper reporters and appearing on television news programs. But none of these interviews did him any good. Conservatives were so outraged at the original news report that they no longer wished to listen to what Koop had to say.

For conservatives, Koop's letter was the last straw, and it irrevocably broke the back of their relationship with him. His attacks on the tobacco industry and his position on AIDS had upset them, but to them his apparent turnabout on abortion represented the ultimate betrayal. After all, Dr. Koop had been chosen and championed by them precisely because of his personal anti-abortion views. Now he was called a traitor to the cause as many conservatives on the Hill attacked his character and morality and accused him of selling out to the pro-choice liberals. The *National Review*, a conservative journal, named Koop as "one of the major disappointments of the Reagan administration."[5] Michael Schwartz, president of the conservative Free Congress Foundation, said of Koop, "I think the guy's a disgrace. . . . He sold out on every one of the principles that made him Surgeon General."[6] And Howard Phillips, chairman of the Conservative Caucus, complained that if Koop "couldn't act on what he believed to be correct, he should have resigned."[7]

Koop was hurt by these attacks, coming as they did from one-time friends. He tried to explain that he had not changed his position on abortion at all, that he still opposed it just as stridently as he always had. "I just refuse to be dishonest with statistics, that's all," Koop said in his defense.[8] But few in the conservative camp listened. Most had already written Koop off, and so had the White House. Bush administration recruiters never contacted Koop, although Koop had made it known that he was interested in the cabinet position of Secretary for Health and Human Services. When Bush named Dr. Louis Sullivan to the post, Koop knew it was his cue to leave.

No one asked him to go, but Koop realized that the Bush White House had no interest in keeping him. A series of petty snubs, such as being denied access to the executive dining room, had made Koop feel unwelcome. White House staffers stopped returning his calls. Then his top aide was fired. Koop decided to resign a few months before his term as Surgeon General officially expired. "It was time," he said.[9] And after eight years of political in-fighting—first with the liberals, and then with the conservatives—Koop was ready to leave. During one of his last interviews before leaving office, a reporter asked the Surgeon General how he had earned the medals on his uniform. "The top row is for what the liberals did to me," Koop told him, "and the bottom row is for what the conservatives did."[10]

As he recovered from the sting of the White House rejection, however, Koop began to realize that even at the age of 72, there were still many opportunities open to him outside the government. Koop realized that during his tenure as Surgeon General he had come to be liked and respected by the American public. The man who eight years earlier had been widely considered a quack was now seen as "America's family doctor." People smiled at him on the street, came up to him to say hello, and thanked him for his good work as Surgeon General. Sometimes people shared very intimate stories. "You made my mother quit smoking, thank you," one stranger told him. "My son died of AIDS," another said. "God bless you."[11] In planning his third career, Koop decided to use this influence to crusade for better health care, only now he would have the added comfort of knowing that he could speak out on public health issues without worrying about the political consequences.

Of course, Koop could have used his celebrity for personal profit. As soon as he resigned, Koop was offered a series of commercial endorsements for everything from condoms to breakfast cereal, but he turned them all down. In one single

Koop's "Safe Kids" campaign works for better pediatric health care.

week, he declined $8 million in offers! But making commercials was not Koop's style. As he later wrote, "I was not about to sell or rent my integrity and the public trust."[12] Instead, Koop took over as chairman of the National "Safe Kids" Campaign, while he wrote articles and made speeches calling for national health care reform.

As Surgeon General, Koop had been unable to tackle the issue of health care reform because it was outside the jurisdiction of his office—and because it had been considered too politically volatile by the Reagan and then the Bush administrations. Now that he was out of government, however, Koop found himself free to lobby for change. He knew firsthand that the United States health care system—the health *scare* system, as Koop called it—was in crisis. In 1990, the United States spent $661 billion on health care—more than the amount spent on defense and education combined—but one in six Americans still had no health care insurance. "There is something terribly wrong," Koop said, "with a system of health care that spends more and more money to serve fewer and fewer people."[13]

Living up to his reputation as a workaholic, Koop toured the country giving speeches on public health issues, hosted his own weekly television show, and in 1991, even published his autobiography entitled *Koop: The Memoirs of America's Family Doctor*. Some months after leaving the government, Koop had been asked by a reporter what he hoped to accomplish in the future. He replied, "I'd like people to say five years from now, `When Koop left the office of Surgeon General, he continued to be the health conscience of America.'" [14]

C. Everett Koop more than lived up to his promise.

Important Events in
C. Everett Koop's Life

1916	Born October 14 in Brooklyn, New York.
1937	Graduates from Dartmouth College.
1938	Marries Betty Flanagan on September 19 in Poughkeepsie, New York.
1941	Graduates from Cornell University Medical College and moves to Philadelphia.
1946	Becomes surgeon-in-chief at the Children's Hospital of Philadelphia.
1968	Writes *Sometimes Mountains Move* after his son David dies in a climbing accident.
1973	The Supreme Court legalizes abortion in the case of *Roe v. Wade*.
1977	Makes history by separating two Siamese twins connected at the heart.
1979	Begins speaking on the anti-abortion circuit.
1980	Ronald Reagan is elected President of the United States.
1981	Is nominated to the post of Surgeon General in March and confirmed in November.
1984	Launches "SFS-2000" campaign.
1986	Writes *The Surgeon General's Report on AIDS*.
1989	Resigns the office of Surgeon General in July.
	Becomes chairman of the National "Safe Kids" Campaign.

Notes

Chapter 1

1. C. Everett Koop, *Koop: The Memoirs of America's Family Doctor* (New York: Random House, 1991), p. 4.
2. John Judis, "An Officer and a Gentleman," *New Republic*, January 23, 1989.
3. Koop, pp. 3-4.
4. *New York Times*, October 14, 1988.
5. Judis, *New Republic*, January 23, 1989.
6. Judis, *New Republic*, January 23, 1989.

Chapter 2

1. Koop, p. 16.
2. Koop, p. 29.
3. Koop, p. 31.
4. Koop, p. 24.
5. Koop, p. 25.

Chapter 3

1. Koop, p. 35.
2. Koop, p. 52.
3. Lynn Rosselini, "Rebel with a Cause," *US News and World Report*, May 30, 1988.
4. Koop, p. 59.

Chapter 4

1. Koop, p. 64.
2. Koop, p. 66.
3. Koop, pp. 71-72.
4. Koop, p. 77.
5. Koop, p. 99.
6. Koop, p. 84.

Chapter 5

1. Koop, p. 99.
2. Koop, p. 109.
3. Koop, p. 90.
4. Rosselini, *US News and World Report*, May 30, 1988.
5. Koop, p. 84.
6. Koop, p. 87.

Chapter 6

1. Koop, p. 262.
2. Koop, p. 132.
3. Koop, p. 142.
4. Koop, p. 7.
5. Philip Yancey, "The Embattled Career of Dr. Koop," *Christianity Today*, October 20, 1989.
6. Yancey, *Christianity Today*, October 20, 1989.
7. Rosselini, *US News and World Report*, May 30, 1988.
8. Yancey, *Christianity Today*, October 20, 1989.

Chapter 7

1. Paul Glastris, "Warning: The Surgeon General May Be Good For Your Health," *Washington Monthly*, March, 1987.

Chapter 8

1. Koop, p. 163.
2. Glastris, *Washington Monthly*, March, 1987.
3. Glastris, *Washington Monthly*, March, 1987.
4. Glastris, *Washington Monthly*, March, 1987.

5. Glastris, *Washington Monthly*, March, 1987.

6. Glastris, *Washington Monthly*, March, 1987.

7. Glastris, *Washington Monthly*, March, 1987.

8. Laurie Jones, "Alcohol Industry Raps Plan to Curb Drunk Driving," *American Medical News*, January 19, 1989.

9. Jones, *American Medical News*, January 19, 1989.

Chapter 9

1. *The New Yorker*, August 7, 1989.

2. Yancey, *Christianity Today*, October 20, 1989.

3. Koop, p. 195.

4. Glastris, *Washington Monthly*, March, 1987.

5. Rosselini, *US News and World Report*, May 30, 1988.

6. Yancey, *Christianity Today*, October 20, 1989.

7. Philip Yancey, *Christianity Today*, November 3, 1989.

8. Glastris, *Washington Monthly*, March, 1987.

9. *New York Times*, August 3, 1988.

10. Glastris, *Washington Monthly*, March, 1987.

11. *New York Times*, August 3, 1988.

12. *New York Times*, August 3, 1988.

13. Ed Doerr, "A Fall From Grace on the Right," *US News and World Report*, May 25, 1987.

14. Margaret Carlson, "A Doctor Prescribes Hard Truth," *Time*, April 24, 1989.

15. "C. Everett Koop: Moralist and Scientist," *The Christian Century*, June 22-29, 1988.

16. Doerr, *US News and World Report*, May 25, 1987.

17. Elizabeth Koop, "In Memory of David Koop," *Saturday Evening Post*, November, 1987.

18. Elizabeth Koop, *Saturday Evening Post*, November, 1987.

Chapter 10

1. Phyllis Schlafly, "Drowning the Surgeon General," *Harper's*, September 15, 1987.

2. Koop, p. 262.

3. Yancey, *Christianity Today*, October 20, 1989.

4. Yancey, *Christianity Today*, October 20, 1989.

5. Yancey, *Christianity Today*, October 20, 1989.

6. Yancey, *Christianity Today*, October 20, 1989.

7. Yancey, *Christianity Today*, October 20, 1989.

8. Yancey, *Christianity Today*, November 3, 1989.

9. Yancey, *Christianity Today*, November 3, 1989.

10. Yancey, *Christianity Today*, October 20, 1989.

11. Koop, p. 315.

12. Koop, p. 316.

13. Koop, p. 302.

14. Jones, *American Medical News*, January 19, 1989.

Suggested Reading

Berger, Gilda. *Smoking Not Allowed: The Debate*. New York: Franklin Watts, 1987.

Check, William. *AIDS*. New York: Chelsea House, 1989.

Durie, Bruce. *Medicine*. Lexington, Mass.: Silver Burdett & Ginn, 1987.

Heintz, Carl. *Medical Ethics*. New York: Franklin Watts, 1987.

Hyde, Margaret O., and Elizabeth H. Forsyth. *AIDS: What Does It Mean to You?* New York: Walker & Co., 1987.

Koop, C. Everett. *Koop: The Memoirs of America's Family Doctor*. New York: Random House, 1991.

Levert, Suzanne. *AIDS: In Search of a Killer*. Englewood Cliffs, N.J.: Julian Messner, 1987.

Ward, Brian. *Smoking and Health*. New York: Franklin Watts, 1986.

Index

Anne Bianchi is the author of *Smart Choices: A Guide for Women Returning to School* and *Tricks*. She has also written extensively on health-related subjects for national publications including *The Christian Science Monitor, Elle, Education Digest,* and *Lear's*. She lives in New York City.